I0837984

Chapter 1: Understanding Depression

Defining Depression

Depression is a complex mental health condition that affects millions of people worldwide, manifesting in a variety of symptoms and experiences. It is often characterized by persistent feelings of sadness, hopelessness, and a lack of interest in activities that once brought joy. This pervasive mood disorder can disrupt daily life, making it difficult to navigate relationships, work, and self-care. Understanding depression is the first step towards managing its impact, especially in the context of personal connections and overall well-being.

The symptoms of depression can vary from person to person and may include emotional, physical, and cognitive changes. Emotional symptoms often involve deep feelings of despair and irritability, while physical symptoms can range from fatigue and changes in appetite to sleep disturbances. Cognitive effects might include difficulty concentrating and making decisions. Recognizing these symptoms is crucial for individuals experiencing depression, as it can validate their feelings and encourage them to seek support and treatment.

One of the significant impacts of depression is its effect on relationships. Those suffering from depression may find it challenging to communicate openly with loved ones, leading to misunderstandings and feelings of isolation. Partners, friends, and family members may struggle to comprehend the emotional weight of depression, which can result in frustration and strain within relationships. It is essential for individuals to express their feelings and educate their loved ones about their experiences, fostering empathy and understanding in the process.

Coping strategies play a vital role in managing depression and its effects on daily life. Nutrition and diet are increasingly recognized for their influence on mental health, with certain foods shown to support brain function and emotional regulation. Mindfulness and meditation techniques can also provide individuals with tools to ground themselves in the present moment, reducing anxiety and promoting emotional stability. Engaging in creative outlets, such as writing or art, allows for the expression of feelings that may be difficult to verbalize, serving as a therapeutic release.

Physical activity is another key component in alleviating depressive symptoms. Regular exercise has been proven to boost mood and improve overall mental health, providing both immediate and long-term benefits. Furthermore, establishing a solid support system, whether through friends, family, or support groups, can significantly impact an individual's journey with depression. Understanding the interplay between sleep and depression is also essential, as poor sleep can exacerbate symptoms, creating a challenging cycle. Ultimately, by addressing these various aspects, individuals can work towards navigating their lives and relationships more effectively, even in the shadow of depression.

Symptoms and Diagnosis

Understanding the symptoms of depression is crucial for those experiencing its effects, as recognition can be the first step toward seeking help. Depression manifests in various ways, including persistent sadness, a sense of hopelessness, and a loss of interest in activities once enjoyed. Individuals may also experience changes in appetite, weight fluctuations, fatigue, difficulty concentrating, or even feelings of worthlessness. These symptoms can vary in intensity and duration, often affecting daily functioning, interpersonal relationships, and overall quality of life. Being aware of these signs can empower individuals to take action, whether that means reaching out for support or exploring coping strategies.

Diagnosing depression involves a comprehensive evaluation by a mental health professional, who will look for specific criteria outlined in diagnostic manuals like the DSM-5. This process typically includes a detailed discussion of symptoms, their duration, and their impact on daily life. A professional may also consider any co-occurring conditions, such as anxiety or substance use disorders, which can complicate the clinical picture. For many, understanding the diagnostic process can reduce feelings of isolation and uncertainty, highlighting that depression is a recognized medical condition that can be treated effectively.

It is essential to differentiate between the symptoms of depression and normal emotional fluctuations. Temporary feelings of sadness or stress do not constitute depression; rather, it is the persistence and depth of these feelings that signal a need for intervention. Individuals should keep track of their mood patterns, noting when symptoms intensify and any potential triggers. This record can be beneficial in discussions with healthcare providers, leading to a more accurate diagnosis and tailored treatment plan. Recognizing the distinction can also alleviate guilt or shame often associated with experiencing depressive symptoms.

Once diagnosed, various treatment options can be explored, including therapy, medication, and lifestyle modifications. Cognitive-behavioral therapy (CBT) has proven effective in helping individuals reframe negative thought patterns, while medications can help balance brain chemistry. Additionally, incorporating nutrition, exercise, and mindfulness practices can significantly enhance treatment outcomes. Understanding that there are multiple pathways to recovery can instill hope and encourage individuals to seek and adhere to a multi-faceted approach tailored to their unique experiences.

Support systems play a vital role in managing depression, particularly in navigating relationships. Open communication with loved ones about symptoms and needs can foster understanding and connection. Joining support groups can also provide a sense of community and shared experience. For parents, discussing the impact of depression on parenting can lead to strategies that prioritize self-care while ensuring that children receive the support they need. By recognizing the symptoms and pursuing a diagnosis, individuals can better equip themselves to cope with the complexities of depression and its effects on their relationships and daily lives.

The Science Behind Depression

Depression is a complex mental health condition characterized by a persistent feeling of sadness and a lack of interest or pleasure in previously enjoyable activities. Understanding the science behind depression can provide valuable insights for individuals grappling with this disorder. Research indicates that depression is not merely a result of negative thinking or personal failure; rather, it involves a combination of genetic, biochemical, environmental, and psychological factors. Neurotransmitters, such as serotonin and dopamine, play a crucial role in mood regulation. An imbalance in these chemicals can lead to the symptoms associated with depression, affecting both emotional and physical well-being.

The impact of depression on relationships can be profound, as the condition often distorts communication and emotional availability. Individuals suffering from depression may withdraw from loved ones, leading to misunderstandings and feelings of isolation for both partners. This withdrawal can create a cycle of disconnection, where the depressed individual feels misunderstood and their partner feels helpless. Understanding the mechanisms of depression can help both parties navigate these challenges with compassion and patience. Recognizing that depression is not a reflection of personal failings can foster an environment of support and healing within relationships.

Nutrition and diet play a significant role in managing depressive symptoms. Research suggests that certain dietary patterns, such as those rich in omega-3 fatty acids, whole grains, and antioxidants, can positively influence mood and overall mental health. Conversely, diets high in processed foods and sugar may exacerbate symptoms of depression. Being mindful of nutritional choices can empower individuals to take an active role in their recovery. Incorporating nutrient-dense foods into daily meals not only supports physical health but also provides the mental clarity and emotional resilience needed to cope with the challenges of depression.

Mindfulness and meditation techniques have gained attention as effective strategies for managing depression. These practices encourage individuals to focus on the present moment, reducing rumination and anxiety about the past or future. Regular engagement in mindfulness exercises can lead to changes in brain function, promoting greater emotional regulation and resilience. For those living with depression, dedicating time to mindfulness can serve as a grounding technique, helping to manage overwhelming feelings and fostering a sense of peace amidst turmoil.

Exercise is another powerful tool in alleviating depressive symptoms. Physical activity stimulates the release of endorphins, often referred to as "feel-good" hormones, which can improve mood and reduce feelings of sadness. Establishing a routine that includes regular exercise, even in small increments, can create a sense of achievement and purpose. Additionally, exercise provides an opportunity to engage with others, which can help combat the isolation often felt during depressive episodes. By understanding the science behind these coping strategies, individuals can better equip themselves to navigate the complexities of depression and its impact on their lives and relationships.

Chapter 2: The impact of depression on relationships

How Depression Affects Communication

Depression significantly alters the way individuals communicate, often creating barriers that can hinder personal and professional relationships. Those experiencing depression may find it challenging to articulate their thoughts and feelings, leading to misunderstandings with loved ones. This difficulty can stem from a variety of factors, including cognitive distortions, fatigue, and a pervasive sense of hopelessness. As a result, what might have been an open dialogue in healthier times can become fraught with silence, miscommunication, or overly simplified responses that do not convey the depth of the individual's feelings.

In many cases, individuals dealing with depression may withdraw from social interactions altogether, fearing judgment or misunderstanding from others. This withdrawal can lead to an isolating cycle—depression fuels the desire to retreat, while the lack of communication exacerbates feelings of loneliness. Friends and family may interpret this behavior as disinterest or rejection, which can further strain relationships. It is crucial for both the individual and their loved ones to recognize that this withdrawal is a symptom of depression rather than a personal choice or failing.

Moreover, nonverbal communication can also be affected by depression. Individuals may exhibit body language that suggests disinterest or fatigue, such as avoiding eye contact, slumped posture, or minimal facial expressions. These signals can be misread by others, leading to further misunderstandings. For those suffering from depression, being aware of these nonverbal cues can be a step toward improving communication. Engaging in mindfulness techniques can help individuals become more attuned to their body language and the messages they are conveying, allowing for more authentic interactions.

Additionally, depression can distort one's perception of conversations. Individuals may interpret neutral statements as negative or feel overly sensitive to criticism, which can lead to defensive responses or withdrawal from conversations altogether. This sensitivity can create a feedback loop that further alienates individuals from their support systems. Practicing mindful reflection and cognitive restructuring can help individuals challenge these distorted thoughts, fostering clearer communication and reducing the emotional burden of misinterpretation.

Finally, creating a supportive environment for open communication is essential in managing the impact of depression on relationships. Encouraging loved ones to ask open-ended questions and express their willingness to listen can help those suffering to feel more comfortable sharing their feelings. Establishing regular check-ins or using creative outlets, such as writing or art, can also facilitate conversations that may be difficult to initiate verbally. Building this foundation of understanding can not only enhance communication but also strengthen relationships, creating a network of support that is vital for navigating the challenges of living with depression.

Changes in Intimacy and Affection

Changes in intimacy and affection are often profound and multifaceted for individuals experiencing depression. This condition can create a barrier between partners, leading to a significant decline in emotional and physical closeness. The persistent feelings of sadness, worthlessness, and fatigue associated with depression can overshadow the desire for intimacy, leaving loved ones feeling rejected or distant. It is essential to recognize that these changes are not a reflection of a partner's feelings but rather a manifestation of the illness itself. Understanding this dynamic can help in navigating the complexities of relationships during difficult times.

As depression takes hold, individuals may withdraw from social interactions and physical connections, leading to misunderstandings within relationships. Partners may feel confused or hurt by the lack of affection, interpreting it as a loss of love or interest. However, it is crucial to communicate openly about these feelings and the impact of depression on one's ability to engage in intimate moments. Establishing a dialogue about changes in affection can foster understanding and empathy, allowing both partners to adapt to the evolving nature of their relationship.

Engaging in coping strategies can also help mitigate the effects of depression on intimacy. Mindfulness and meditation can enhance emotional awareness, making it easier to express feelings and needs. These practices encourage individuals to be present and attuned to their emotions, which can lead to more meaningful interactions with partners. Additionally, incorporating creative outlets, such as journaling or art, can provide a space for expressing feelings that may be difficult to verbalize. This expression can bridge the gap in intimacy by fostering a deeper understanding between partners.

Nutrition and physical health play a significant role in managing depression, which can indirectly influence intimacy. A balanced diet can improve mood stability, while regular exercise is known to release endorphins, enhancing overall feelings of well-being. When individuals prioritize their physical health, they may find it easier to engage in affectionate behaviors and maintain emotional connections. Encouraging each other to partake in physical activities together, such as walking or yoga, can also serve as a means to reconnect and strengthen the bond between partners.

Support systems are critical in navigating changes in intimacy and affection. Reaching out to friends, family, or support groups can provide individuals with the encouragement they need to address their struggles with depression openly. These networks can offer insights and strategies that help partners understand and adapt to the changes in their relationship. Ultimately, fostering an environment where both partners feel safe to discuss their feelings and challenges can lead to a more resilient and compassionate connection, even in the face of depression.

The Strain on Family Dynamics

The strain on family dynamics due to depression can be profound and multifaceted. Family members often experience a range of emotions, from frustration and confusion to sadness and helplessness. As depression alters an individual's behavior and mood, it may lead to misunderstandings and miscommunications within the family unit. Loved ones may feel isolated, struggling to comprehend the changes in the depressed individual, which can exacerbate feelings of alienation and distress. This disruption can create a cycle where the family environment becomes more tense, making it even harder for the individual suffering from depression to seek support.

Effective communication is essential in navigating these challenges. Family members should strive to express their feelings and concerns openly, creating a safe space where everyone can share their experiences without fear of judgment. Encouraging discussions about emotions can help normalize the feelings surrounding depression, allowing family members to better understand one another's perspectives. It's also crucial to listen actively, acknowledging the struggles faced by the individual with depression. This two-way communication fosters empathy and can bridge the emotional gap that depression often creates.

Incorporating coping strategies into daily life can greatly benefit the entire family. Establishing routines that emphasize healthy eating, regular exercise, and mindfulness can create a supportive environment conducive to recovery. Family members can participate in these activities together, promoting bonding and shared experiences. For instance, preparing nutritious meals as a family can instill a sense of togetherness while also addressing dietary needs associated with managing depression. Similarly, engaging in physical activities can serve as both a therapeutic outlet and a way to alleviate depressive symptoms collectively.

Creative outlets can also play a significant role in healing family dynamics. Encouraging artistic expression, whether through writing, painting, or music, can provide family members with a constructive way to communicate their feelings. This form of expression not only helps individuals cope with their own emotional turmoil but can also enhance understanding among family members. By sharing creative works, family members can gain insights into each other's experiences and struggles, fostering a deeper connection and compassion for one another.

Finally, establishing a supportive network is critical for families dealing with depression. This network can include extended family, friends, and mental health professionals, who can offer guidance and reassurance. Seeking support together can not only alleviate some of the burdens of depression but also strengthen family bonds. By recognizing that they are not alone in this journey, families can work collaboratively toward healing, ultimately transforming the strain into a source of resilience and unity.

Chapter 3: Coping Strategies for Daily Life with Depression

Establishing a Routine

Establishing a routine can be a vital component in managing depression and improving overall well-being. For individuals grappling with depressive symptoms, the unpredictability of daily life can exacerbate feelings of hopelessness and disconnection. A structured routine can provide a sense of stability and predictability, allowing individuals to regain a sense of control over their lives. By incorporating specific practices into daily schedules, individuals can create a foundation that supports both mental health and their relationships with others.

When developing a routine, it is important to focus on small, manageable goals. Breaking down tasks into bite-sized pieces can prevent feelings of overwhelm that often accompany depression. For example, instead of aiming to clean an entire house, one might set a goal to tidy just one room each day. This approach not only makes tasks feel more achievable but also fosters a sense of accomplishment, which can be uplifting. As individuals begin to experience small successes, they may find it easier to engage in other aspects of life, including maintaining relationships.

Nutrition plays a crucial role in mental health, and incorporating healthy eating habits into a daily routine is essential. Establishing regular meal times can help regulate mood and energy levels. Preparing balanced meals that include essential nutrients can contribute to improved mental clarity and emotional stability. Additionally, involving family members or friends in meal preparation can serve as a social activity that strengthens bonds and provides support. Sharing meals together can enhance connections and create opportunities for open discussions about feelings and experiences.

Mindfulness and meditation practices can also be integrated into a daily routine to promote emotional resilience. Setting aside time each day for mindfulness exercises or meditation can help individuals cultivate a sense of peace and awareness. These practices encourage individuals to focus on the present moment, which can reduce rumination and anxiety often associated with depression. Engaging in mindfulness as part of a routine can facilitate deeper connections with oneself and others, encouraging healthier interactions in relationships.

Finally, incorporating physical activity into a daily schedule can significantly alleviate depressive symptoms. Exercise releases endorphins, which are natural mood lifters. Whether it's a brisk walk, yoga, or a dance class, finding ways to stay active can invigorate both the body and mind. Establishing a routine that includes regular physical activity can also provide opportunities for social engagement, whether through group classes or exercising with friends. As individuals prioritize their physical health, they may find that their emotional well-being improves, fostering stronger relationships and a greater sense of fulfillment in life.

Setting Realistic Goals

Setting realistic goals is a vital strategy for individuals coping with depression, as it can provide a sense of direction and accomplishment. When experiencing depression, the weight of daily tasks can feel overwhelming, leading to feelings of inadequacy and frustration. By establishing achievable goals, individuals can cultivate a sense of progress, which is essential for enhancing motivation and improving overall mental health. These goals should be specific, measurable, and tailored to one's current emotional capacity, ensuring they are attainable without adding further stress.

To begin, it is crucial to break down larger aspirations into smaller, manageable steps. For instance, instead of aiming to overhaul one's entire diet in a week, start by incorporating one healthy meal or snack each day. This incremental approach not only eases the pressure but also allows for gradual adaptation to new habits. Celebrating small victories, such as completing a single task or making a healthier choice, can provide positive reinforcement, contributing to a more positive self-image and countering the negative thought patterns often associated with depression.

In the context of relationships, setting realistic goals can significantly enhance communication and connection with loved ones. Rather than expecting to resolve deep-seated issues in one conversation, focus on having open dialogues about feelings and needs in smaller, more manageable interactions. This can help build trust and understanding, facilitating a supportive environment where both partners feel heard and valued. Additionally, involving partners in goal-setting can strengthen the bond, as they may offer support and encouragement, further alleviating the sense of isolation that often accompanies depression.

Mindfulness and meditation techniques can be integrated into goal-setting practices to foster a more compassionate approach towards oneself. By being present and acknowledging one's feelings without judgment, individuals can gain clarity on what they genuinely want to achieve. This self-awareness allows for the establishment of goals that resonate personally, rather than those imposed by societal expectations or external pressures. Incorporating short mindfulness sessions into daily routines can also help in alleviating anxiety about achieving these goals, promoting a more balanced mindset.

Finally, understanding the role of external support systems is crucial in the goal-setting process. Engaging with therapists, support groups, or friends can provide valuable insights and encouragement. They can help in refining goals and holding individuals accountable in a gentle manner. Additionally, sharing goals with others can foster a sense of community and belonging, which is especially beneficial for those navigating the challenges of depression. Ultimately, setting realistic goals not only enhances personal growth but also nurtures relationships, paving the way for a more hopeful and fulfilling life.

Journaling and Self-Reflection

Journaling and self-reflection can serve as powerful tools for individuals navigating the complex landscape of depression. Engaging in regular journaling provides an outlet for thoughts and emotions that may feel overwhelming or difficult to express verbally. By putting pen to paper, individuals can clarify their feelings, identify patterns in their mood, and track their emotional responses to various situations. This practice not only fosters self-awareness but also encourages a deeper understanding of the triggers and influences that affect one's mental health, ultimately enabling better coping strategies in daily life.

Through self-reflection, journaling can also enhance relationships that may be strained by depression. Writing about interactions with loved ones allows individuals to explore their feelings about these relationships and the ways their depression may impact others. This process can lead to more effective communication, as it helps articulate feelings that might otherwise remain unspoken. By examining thoughts and emotions in a safe space, individuals can prepare themselves for difficult conversations, fostering a more supportive environment for both themselves and their partners or family members.

In addition to emotional exploration, journaling can serve as a creative outlet for expressing feelings associated with depression. Creative writing, poetry, or even doodling can provide a means to convey experiences that may seem too complex for straightforward language. This creative expression can be therapeutic, offering relief and a sense of accomplishment. Moreover, it can help individuals connect with their inner selves, promoting a sense of identity that is often overshadowed by depressive symptoms.

Incorporating mindfulness into journaling practices can further enhance its benefits. Mindful journaling encourages individuals to focus on the present moment, acknowledging their thoughts and feelings without judgment. This approach not only aids in reducing anxiety but also fosters a sense of calm and clarity. By combining mindfulness techniques with journaling, individuals can develop a more compassionate view of themselves, allowing for healing and growth in both personal and relational contexts.

Ultimately, journaling and self-reflection can play a vital role in managing depression and improving relationships. By providing a structured way to process emotions, individuals can cultivate greater self-awareness, enhance their communication skills, and tap into their creative potential. As these practices become integrated into daily routines, they can serve as a foundation for developing healthier coping mechanisms, strengthening support systems, and fostering a more profound connection with oneself and others.

Chapter 4: Nutrition and Diet for Managing Depression

The Role of Nutrition in Mental Health

The connection between nutrition and mental health has garnered significant attention in recent years, particularly in the context of managing depression. The foods we consume have a profound effect on our brain chemistry and overall mood. Nutritional deficiencies can exacerbate depressive symptoms, while a balanced diet can serve as a powerful ally in the journey toward emotional stability. Essential nutrients such as omega-3 fatty acids, B vitamins, and minerals like magnesium and zinc play crucial roles in the production of neurotransmitters that regulate mood, highlighting the importance of dietary choices in mental health management.

Incorporating a variety of whole foods into one's diet can significantly improve mental well-being. Fruits, vegetables, whole grains, lean proteins, and healthy fats provide the necessary vitamins and minerals that support brain function. For individuals dealing with depression, the shift from processed foods, which often contain high levels of sugars and unhealthy fats, to nutrient-dense options can lead to noticeable improvements in mood. Foods rich in antioxidants, such as berries and leafy greens, can help reduce inflammation in the body, which is linked to mood disorders. By prioritizing whole foods, individuals may experience enhanced energy levels and mental clarity.

Moreover, the timing of meals and snacks can also influence mood and energy levels throughout the day. Regular meal patterns help maintain stable blood sugar levels, which can prevent mood swings and irritability. Mindful eating practices, where individuals focus on the sensory experience of eating, can foster a deeper connection to food and enhance the enjoyment of meals. This approach not only encourages healthier dietary choices but also promotes a sense of calm and awareness, which can be particularly beneficial for those navigating the challenges of depression.

Hydration is another critical aspect of nutrition that should not be overlooked. Dehydration can lead to fatigue, confusion, and irritability, all of which can exacerbate depressive symptoms. Drinking adequate amounts of water throughout the day can help maintain optimal brain function and emotional balance. Additionally, certain herbal teas, such as chamomile or peppermint, can contribute to relaxation and stress relief, offering a simple yet effective way to support mental health through dietary choices.

Finally, it is essential to recognize that while nutrition plays a vital role in mental health, it is just one piece of a larger puzzle. A holistic approach that includes mindfulness, exercise, and support systems is crucial for managing depression effectively. Encouraging individuals to seek professional guidance from nutritionists or mental health practitioners can enhance their understanding of how diet impacts mental health and relationships. By weaving together these various aspects of self-care, individuals can cultivate a more balanced and fulfilling life, even in the shadows of depression.

Foods that Boost Mood

Foods that have the potential to boost mood can play a significant role in managing depression and improving overall well-being. The relationship between diet and mental health has garnered considerable attention in recent years, with various studies highlighting how specific nutrients can influence mood and emotional health. Incorporating these foods into your daily routine can be a practical coping strategy for those navigating the challenges of depression, potentially providing both psychological relief and physical nourishment.

One category of mood-boosting foods includes those rich in omega-3 fatty acids, such as fatty fish, walnuts, and flaxseeds. Omega-3s are known for their anti-inflammatory properties and their role in brain health. Research suggests that individuals who consume higher amounts of omega-3 fatty acids tend to report lower levels of depression. Including these foods in your diet can not only support cognitive function but also promote a more balanced emotional state, thereby enhancing interpersonal relationships that may be strained due to depressive symptoms.

Another important group of foods includes those high in complex carbohydrates, such as whole grains, legumes, and vegetables. Complex carbohydrates help regulate serotonin levels in the brain, a neurotransmitter that plays a crucial role in mood stabilization. By opting for whole grain bread, brown rice, and oats over refined carbohydrates, individuals can experience more sustained energy levels and mood improvements. These dietary choices can also aid in reducing irritability and anxiety, which are common issues for those living with depression and can significantly impact relationships with family, friends, and coworkers.

Fruits and vegetables, particularly those rich in vitamins and antioxidants—such as berries, citrus fruits, spinach, and kale—are essential for maintaining mental health. They help combat oxidative stress and inflammation, which are often elevated in individuals suffering from depression. A diet abundant in colorful fruits and vegetables can provide the necessary nutrients to support brain health while also offering a creative outlet through meal preparation and planning. Engaging in cooking and experimenting with new recipes can serve as a form of mindfulness practice, contributing positively to emotional well-being.

Lastly, foods containing probiotics, like yogurt, kefir, and fermented vegetables, can play a significant role in gut health, which has been increasingly linked to mental health. The gut-brain connection is an area of growing research, suggesting that a healthy gut can positively affect mood and emotional regulation. Incorporating probiotic-rich foods into your diet can not only enhance digestive health but potentially improve the symptoms of depression, thereby fostering a more stable emotional environment. By making conscious dietary choices, individuals can take proactive steps toward managing their depression and improving their relationships.

Meal Planning for Emotional Well-being

Meal planning can serve as a valuable tool for individuals navigating the complexities of depression. The act of preparing meals not only ensures that nutritious food is available but also fosters a sense of control and accomplishment. When depression weighs heavily, it can be challenging to prioritize self-care, including nutrition. By establishing a structured meal plan, individuals can create a framework that supports their emotional well-being and can help mitigate some symptoms of depression. This approach transforms the often overwhelming task of daily meals into manageable steps, making it easier to maintain a healthy diet.

Incorporating nutrient-rich foods into daily meals is crucial for managing depression. Studies have shown that certain nutrients, such as omega-3 fatty acids, B vitamins, and antioxidants, can positively influence mood and cognitive function. Meal planning allows individuals to focus on including these beneficial foods, such as fatty fish, leafy greens, nuts, and whole grains, into their diets. By consciously choosing ingredients that nourish the body and mind, individuals can enhance their overall well-being and create a more positive emotional environment.

Additionally, meal planning can offer a sense of mindfulness, an important aspect of managing depression. The process of selecting recipes, preparing ingredients, and cooking can serve as a form of meditation, allowing individuals to engage their senses and immerse themselves in the present moment. This mindfulness practice can act as a distraction from negative thoughts and feelings, providing a brief reprieve. Taking time to appreciate the colors, textures, and aromas of food can cultivate a deeper connection with oneself and promote emotional regulation.

Social connections can also be reinforced through meal planning. Sharing meals with loved ones can strengthen relationships and create opportunities for open dialogue. When individuals invite friends or family members to participate in meal preparation or join them for a meal, it fosters a supportive environment that can combat feelings of isolation. This communal aspect of eating not only nourishes the body but also uplifts the spirit, reminding those affected by depression that they are not alone in their struggles.

Lastly, meal planning can contribute to better sleep hygiene, which is often disrupted by depression. Consuming a balanced diet helps regulate hormones and maintain energy levels, ultimately benefiting sleep quality. By planning meals that are rich in magnesium, tryptophan, and other sleep-promoting nutrients, individuals can enhance their nightly rest. Improved sleep can lead to better mood regulation and increased resilience against depressive symptoms, creating a positive feedback loop that supports both mental health and interpersonal relationships.

Chapter 5: Mindfulness and Meditation Techniques for Depression

Introduction to Mindfulness

Mindfulness is a practice that encourages individuals to focus their attention on the present moment, acknowledging thoughts and feelings without judgment. For those suffering from depression, this approach can be particularly beneficial. It allows individuals to cultivate awareness of their internal experiences, reducing the tendency to ruminate on negative thoughts that often accompany depressive states. By grounding oneself in the present, mindfulness can help break the cycle of despair, creating space for more balanced emotions and thoughts.

Engaging in mindfulness can also foster a greater understanding of how depression impacts relationships. Many people with depression may feel isolated or misunderstood, which can strain connections with loved ones. Mindfulness encourages open communication and presence, allowing individuals to express their feelings more clearly and listen actively to others. This practice can help improve empathy and support within relationships, enabling both partners to navigate the complexities of depression together.

Incorporating mindfulness into daily routines can enhance overall well-being and serve as a coping strategy for managing the symptoms of depression. Simple techniques like mindful breathing or body scanning can be practiced at any time, offering immediate relief from overwhelming emotions. These strategies not only help in managing stress but also promote a healthier perspective on daily challenges, allowing individuals to approach life with a sense of calm and acceptance rather than fear and anxiety.

Mindfulness is also closely linked with nutrition and self-care, as paying attention to one's body and mind can influence dietary choices and overall health. Mindful eating encourages individuals to savor their food, recognize hunger cues, and appreciate the nourishment they provide. This practice can significantly impact mood and energy levels, which are crucial for managing depression. Additionally, being mindful about nutrition can enhance motivation to engage in exercise, further alleviating depressive symptoms through physical activity.

For those parenting while living with depression, mindfulness can serve as a powerful tool to improve both personal well-being and parenting dynamics. Practicing mindfulness allows parents to model emotional regulation and presence for their children, fostering a nurturing environment. It also aids in creating moments of connection amidst the challenges of depression, encouraging parents to engage fully with their children and establish a supportive atmosphere. By integrating mindfulness into daily life, individuals can build resilience and strengthen relationships, all while navigating the complexities of living with depression.

Guided Meditation Practices

Guided meditation practices offer a valuable tool for individuals coping with depression, providing a structured approach to mindfulness that can ease emotional distress and foster a sense of connection. These practices involve listening to a recorded meditation or following a live guide who leads participants through a series of relaxation techniques, visualizations, and breathing exercises. This gentle guidance allows individuals to focus their minds, reducing the overwhelming sensations often associated with depression. By creating a safe space for self-reflection, guided meditation can help individuals cultivate awareness of their thoughts and feelings, leading to deeper insights into their emotional states.

Engaging in guided meditation regularly can yield significant benefits for relationships impacted by depression. Many individuals suffering from depressive symptoms may find it challenging to communicate their feelings or engage fully with loved ones. Through meditation, one can develop a greater sense of emotional regulation, which can enhance interpersonal interactions. As individuals learn to observe their thoughts without judgment, they can approach conversations with more clarity and compassion, creating a more supportive environment for both themselves and their partners. This improved emotional intelligence can help repair and strengthen relationships that might have been strained by the challenges of depression.

Incorporating guided meditation into a daily routine can also complement other coping strategies, such as nutrition and exercise, which are vital in managing depression. By fostering a sense of calm and clarity, meditation can promote healthier eating habits and encourage individuals to engage in physical activity. When the mind is quieted, it becomes easier to recognize the body's needs, paving the way for mindful eating and exercise choices. This holistic approach to mental health can significantly enhance overall well-being, establishing a foundation for resilience in the face of depressive episodes.

For those navigating the complexities of parenting while living with depression, guided meditation can serve as a vital self-care practice. Parenting demands significant emotional energy, and the stress of managing depressive symptoms can make it even more challenging. By dedicating time each day to guided meditation, parents can cultivate patience and mindfulness, which are essential for nurturing their children. This practice not only benefits the parent but also creates a more harmonious atmosphere for the children, who can sense the calm and stability that meditation brings into the home.

Lastly, guided meditation practices can serve as a bridge to building supportive connections with others. Many meditation sessions can be found in group settings, whether in-person or online, fostering community and shared experiences among individuals facing similar challenges. This sense of belonging can provide critical emotional support and reduce feelings of isolation, which are often intensified by depression. By participating in guided meditation within a group, individuals can share their journeys, learn from one another, and develop a support system that is essential for recovery and resilience.

Breathing Exercises for Stress Relief

Breathing exercises are a powerful tool for managing stress, particularly for those experiencing the weight of depression. When feelings of anxiety and hopelessness arise, the body's natural response is often to tense up, which can exacerbate depressive symptoms. Engaging in systematic breathing techniques can help to counteract this physical response, promoting a sense of calm and grounding. Simple exercises can be practiced anywhere and require no special equipment, making them accessible for anyone looking to alleviate stress throughout their day.

One effective technique is known as diaphragmatic breathing, or abdominal breathing. This method encourages deeper breaths that engage the diaphragm rather than shallow chest breathing. To practice, find a comfortable position and place one hand on your chest and the other on your abdomen. Inhale deeply through your nose, allowing your abdomen to rise while keeping your chest relatively still. Hold the breath for a moment, then exhale slowly through your mouth. This process not only helps deliver more oxygen to your body but also activates the parasympathetic nervous system, which promotes relaxation and reduces feelings of anxiety.

Another beneficial exercise is the 4-7-8 technique, which can be particularly useful when facing overwhelming stress or racing thoughts. To perform this exercise, begin by exhaling completely through your mouth. Then, close your mouth and inhale quietly through your nose for a count of four. Hold the breath for a count of seven, and finally, exhale completely through your mouth for a count of eight. This rhythmic breathing pattern helps to regulate the heartbeat, slows down the mind, and creates a feeling of tranquility, which can be especially soothing during moments of depressive episodes.

Incorporating breathing exercises into daily routines can also foster mindfulness, allowing individuals to become more aware of their thoughts and feelings. By setting aside just a few minutes each day for focused breathing, individuals can create a mental space that encourages self-reflection and emotional processing. This practice can lead to increased clarity in relationships, as it allows for more thoughtful responses rather than reactive behaviors that may arise from stress or overwhelm.

Finally, breathing exercises can serve as a bridge to other coping strategies, such as meditation or yoga. The calm induced by focused breathing can enhance the effectiveness of these practices, further alleviating symptoms of depression and improving emotional regulation. By integrating breathing techniques into a broader self-care regimen, individuals can support their mental health and enhance their ability to connect with others, fostering healthier relationships despite the challenges posed by depression.

Chapter 6: Creative Outlets for Expressing Feelings of Depression

Art as a Form of Expression

Art serves as a profound and multifaceted form of expression, particularly for individuals grappling with depression. When words often fail to convey the depths of one's feelings, art can bridge that gap, allowing for the exploration and communication of emotions in a tangible way. This creative outlet can manifest in various forms, including painting, writing, music, dance, and more. Each medium offers a unique way to channel feelings of sadness, isolation, and despair, transforming them into something that can be shared or understood, even if only by oneself. Engaging in artistic activities can also provide a sense of control and agency in a world where many aspects may feel overwhelming.

For those living with depression, the act of creating art can serve as a powerful coping strategy. It allows individuals to process and externalize their emotions, providing an opportunity to reflect on their experiences. This creative process can be meditative, helping to quiet the mind and focus on the moment. Whether it's the rhythmic strokes of a brush on canvas or the cathartic release of writing poetry, art can act as a therapeutic tool that fosters mindfulness. Engaging in such activities can bring a sense of accomplishment, which is particularly crucial for those who often feel stuck or unmotivated.

Moreover, art can play a significant role in relationships impacted by depression. Sharing one's artistic endeavors with loved ones can open up lines of communication that might otherwise remain closed. It invites empathy and understanding, creating a space where partners, friends, or family members can engage with the emotional landscape of the artist. This sharing can lead to deeper connections, as it encourages dialogue about feelings that might be too challenging to articulate verbally. In this way, art not only serves as a personal outlet but also as a bridge that can strengthen interpersonal bonds.

In addition to fostering communication, art can also help combat the feelings of isolation that often accompany depression. Participating in group art classes or workshops can provide social interaction and a sense of community. Being around others who share similar struggles can reduce feelings of loneliness and promote a sense of belonging. These shared experiences can cultivate supportive relationships, which are vital for anyone navigating the complexities of depression. Finding a group of like-minded individuals can also inspire creativity and encourage the exploration of new artistic techniques that might further enhance emotional expression.

Finally, the role of art in managing depression should not be underestimated when considering overall well-being. Engaging in creative activities can stimulate the production of endorphins and other positive neurotransmitters, contributing to improved mood and emotional health. Incorporating art into daily routines can serve as a form of self-care that complements other strategies, such as exercise, nutrition, and mindfulness practices. By embracing artistic expression, individuals can find solace and empowerment, transforming their struggles with depression into a source of creativity and hope for themselves and their relationships.

Writing and Poetry

Writing and poetry serve as powerful tools for individuals grappling with depression, offering a unique avenue to process emotions and articulate experiences that may often feel overwhelming. When words flow onto the page, they can transform chaotic thoughts and feelings into structured expressions, providing a sense of clarity and relief. Engaging in writing allows for introspection, enabling individuals to explore the depths of their emotions without judgment. This act of creation not only fosters self-awareness but can also serve as a therapeutic exercise, helping to untangle the complexities of depression.

For many, poetry becomes a poignant medium to convey feelings that may be difficult to express verbally. The rhythmic nature of poetry can provide a soothing escape, allowing for an exploration of sorrow, longing, and hope. Through metaphors and imagery, poets can encapsulate their inner struggles in a way that resonates with others, creating a shared understanding. This connection can be incredibly validating for those with depression, as it reminds them they are not alone in their experiences. Writing poetry can also foster a sense of accomplishment, reinforcing the idea that their voice matters and can impact others.

Incorporating writing into daily routines can serve as a coping mechanism that enhances mental well-being. Keeping a journal allows individuals to document their thoughts and feelings, which can be particularly beneficial during challenging times. This practice can create a safe space to release pent-up emotions, track patterns in mood, and reflect on personal growth. By establishing a regular writing habit, individuals can develop a sense of stability amidst the unpredictable nature of depression, integrating this creative outlet into their self-care regimen.

Additionally, the act of writing can facilitate communication in relationships affected by depression. Many people find it difficult to articulate their feelings to loved ones, leading to misunderstandings and a sense of isolation. Writing letters or notes can bridge this gap, offering a way to express thoughts and emotions without the pressure of immediate conversation. This written communication can help partners, friends, and family understand the struggles faced by the individual, fostering empathy and support. As relationships grow stronger through this shared understanding, the stigma surrounding depression may begin to dissipate.

Ultimately, writing and poetry can empower individuals living with depression, transforming their pain into art and connection. By embracing these creative outlets, they can navigate the complexities of their emotions, enhance their relationships, and cultivate a deeper understanding of themselves. The written word can become a source of healing, allowing individuals to confront their struggles while simultaneously celebrating their resilience. In this way, writing and poetry not only serve as coping strategies but also as profound expressions of the human experience, particularly in the shadow of depression.

Music and Movement

Music and movement serve as powerful tools for individuals coping with depression, offering an avenue for expression and emotional release. Engaging with music can evoke a range of emotions, helping individuals process feelings that might otherwise remain unexpressed. Listening to uplifting or soothing melodies can create a shift in mood, providing temporary relief from the heaviness of depressive thoughts. Additionally, creating music, whether through singing, playing an instrument, or songwriting, allows for a deeper exploration of one's emotions, fostering a sense of connection to oneself.

Movement, particularly through dance or simple physical activity, complements the benefits of music. The act of moving to a rhythm can stimulate the release of endorphins, the body's natural mood enhancers. This physical response can counteract the lethargy often experienced in depression. Even gentle movements, such as stretching or walking, when paired with music, can enhance emotional well-being and reduce feelings of isolation. These activities not only promote physical health but also create a space for mindfulness, encouraging individuals to focus on the present moment rather than overwhelming thoughts.

Incorporating music and movement into daily routines can serve as a coping strategy for managing depressive symptoms. Setting aside time for a daily dance session or a leisurely walk with music can establish a sense of structure and purpose. This routine can be particularly beneficial for those who struggle with motivation, as the combination of music and movement can act as an encouraging force to get moving. The rhythm and lyrics of songs can resonate with personal experiences, making the act of engaging with them a form of validation and self-acknowledgment.

Furthermore, music and movement can play a significant role in enhancing relationships affected by depression. Shared musical experiences, such as attending concerts or simply dancing together at home, can strengthen bonds between partners, friends, or family members. These activities can create moments of joy and connection, counteracting the feelings of alienation that often accompany depression. By inviting loved ones to partake in these experiences, individuals can foster understanding and support, transforming what can be a solitary struggle into a shared journey of healing.

Lastly, integrating music and movement into parenting while living with depression can provide both parents and children with tools for emotional expression and connection. Engaging in musical activities or playful movement allows parents to model healthy coping strategies for their children. It creates an environment where emotions can be expressed openly and joy can be found, even amidst challenges. By prioritizing these forms of expression, parents can cultivate a nurturing atmosphere that promotes resilience, understanding, and love, essential for both their own well-being and that of their children.

Chapter 7: The Role of Exercise in Alleviating Depressive Symptoms

Understanding the Connection Between Exercise and Mood

Exercise has long been recognized for its physical benefits, but its impact on mood and mental health is equally significant, especially for individuals grappling with depression. Engaging in regular physical activity can stimulate the production of endorphins, which are chemicals in the brain that act as natural painkillers and mood elevators. This biological response can lead to what is often referred to as the "runner's high," a temporary feeling of euphoria and a reduction in feelings of anxiety and depression. For those living with depression, understanding this connection can serve as a powerful motivation to incorporate exercise into their daily routines.

Moreover, exercise has been shown to reduce levels of the body's stress hormones, such as cortisol. High levels of cortisol can exacerbate feelings of anxiety and depression, creating a vicious cycle that can be difficult to break. By participating in physical activities, individuals can not only decrease these harmful hormone levels but also help regulate their mood. This regulation is particularly important for those who may find themselves feeling overwhelmed by their emotions, as consistent exercise can provide a natural and constructive outlet for stress and frustration.

In addition to the biochemical changes that occur during exercise, participating in physical activities can also provide crucial social benefits. For individuals with depression, isolation can be a significant barrier to recovery. Engaging in group exercises or sports can foster a sense of community and support, which is vital for emotional well-being. Whether it's joining a local gym, participating in a yoga class, or simply walking in a park with a friend, these interactions can reduce feelings of loneliness and strengthen social connections that are essential for emotional resilience.

Establishing a consistent exercise routine also promotes a sense of accomplishment and boosts self-esteem. For those battling depression, even small achievements can have a profound impact on their view of themselves and their capabilities. Completing a workout or setting and achieving fitness goals can help shift the focus away from negative thoughts and foster a more positive self-image. This shift can be particularly beneficial in navigating relationships, as improved self-esteem can enhance interpersonal interactions and reduce feelings of inadequacy or guilt that often accompany depression.

Ultimately, understanding the connection between exercise and mood is not just about physical health; it is about nurturing the mind and spirit as well. Incorporating movement into daily life can be a vital coping strategy for managing depression, offering a pathway to improved mental health. By recognizing the multifaceted benefits of exercise, individuals can take proactive steps towards enhancing their mood and, consequently, their relationships with others. This holistic approach to mental health can empower those suffering from depression to reclaim their lives and foster deeper connections with the world around them.

Types of Exercise Beneficial for Depression

Exercise has long been recognized as a powerful tool in the management of depression. Various types of exercise can provide unique benefits, making it crucial for individuals suffering from depression to find an activity that resonates with them. Aerobic activities, such as running, cycling, or swimming, are particularly effective in releasing endorphins, the body's natural mood lifters. Engaging in these exercises can significantly reduce feelings of sadness and anxiety, promoting a sense of well-being. Additionally, maintaining a routine of aerobic exercises can enhance overall physical health, which is often compromised during depressive episodes.

Strength training is another beneficial form of exercise. It not only improves physical strength and endurance but also plays a vital role in boosting self-esteem and confidence. For individuals dealing with depression, the empowerment gained through achieving fitness goals can lead to improved mental health. Furthermore, strength training has been shown to reduce symptoms of anxiety and stress, making it a valuable component of a comprehensive treatment plan for those struggling with their mental health.

Mind-body exercises, such as yoga and tai chi, offer a holistic approach to managing depression. These practices combine physical movement with mental focus and breath control, helping individuals connect their body and mind. The meditative aspects of these exercises can promote relaxation and mindfulness, which are essential for managing depressive symptoms. Regular participation in mind-body exercises can lead to increased self-awareness and emotional regulation, which are crucial for navigating the emotional challenges of depression.

Group exercises can also provide social support, which is particularly beneficial for individuals facing depression. Activities like group fitness classes or team sports foster a sense of belonging and community, reducing feelings of isolation that often accompany mental health struggles. The camaraderie developed in these settings can enhance motivation and accountability, encouraging individuals to maintain their exercise routines. Engaging with others who share similar experiences can also lead to the exchange of coping strategies and emotional support.

Lastly, incorporating physical activity into daily routines, such as walking or engaging in household chores, can have a positive impact on mental health. These small, manageable forms of exercise can help break the cycle of inactivity that often accompanies depression. By integrating movement into everyday tasks, individuals can cultivate a sense of accomplishment and build momentum toward more structured forms of exercise. Ultimately, the key to leveraging exercise as a tool for managing depression lies in finding enjoyable activities that fit seamlessly into one's lifestyle.

Creating an Exercise Routine

Creating an exercise routine can be an essential step in managing depression and improving overall well-being. Regular physical activity has been shown to release endorphins, which are natural mood lifters. For individuals dealing with depression, establishing a consistent exercise routine can provide a sense of accomplishment and structure, helping to combat feelings of hopelessness and lethargy. It is important to understand that the goal is not to create an intense workout plan but rather to find enjoyable and manageable activities that can be incorporated into daily life.

When designing an exercise routine, start by identifying activities that you genuinely enjoy. This could range from walking in nature, dancing to your favorite music, or practicing yoga. The key is to choose exercises that feel less like a chore and more like a source of joy or relaxation. Consider setting small, achievable goals, such as a 10-minute walk each day, gradually increasing the duration and intensity as you feel more comfortable. This incremental approach can help build confidence and motivation, making it easier to stick with the routine over time.

Incorporating exercise into your daily life can also enhance the quality of your relationships. Engaging in physical activities with friends or loved ones can foster connection and support, helping to alleviate feelings of isolation often experienced during depressive episodes. Group classes, outdoor activities, or simply inviting a friend for a walk can strengthen bonds while promoting mental health. Remember, sharing these experiences can create an environment of encouragement and accountability, making it easier to maintain your routine.

Mindfulness can play a significant role in your exercise routine. Focusing on the present moment while engaging in physical activity can enhance the benefits of exercise. Techniques such as deep breathing, paying attention to your body's movements, or appreciating the surroundings can transform a simple workout into a mindful practice. This approach not only helps reduce stress but also allows for a deeper connection with your body, promoting a more positive self-image and emotional resilience.

Lastly, it is crucial to listen to your body and adjust your routine as needed. On days when depression feels overwhelming, it is okay to modify your exercise plan or take a rest day. The goal is to create a sustainable routine that honors your mental health needs. Celebrate your progress, no matter how small, and remember that consistency is more important than intensity. By prioritizing regular exercise, you can cultivate a healthier relationship with yourself, ultimately benefiting your relationships with others.

Chapter 8: Navigating Work and Career Challenges with Depression

Managing Workplace Stress

Managing workplace stress is a crucial aspect of navigating daily life with depression. For individuals suffering from depression, the workplace can often be a source of added pressure and anxiety. It is vital to identify stressors early on and implement effective coping strategies. Recognizing triggers, such as tight deadlines, difficult interpersonal dynamics, or overwhelming workloads, can help individuals take proactive steps to mitigate their effects. Creating a structured daily schedule can also provide a sense of control and predictability, which is particularly beneficial for those dealing with mood fluctuations.

Incorporating mindfulness and meditation techniques into the workday can significantly reduce stress levels. Simple practices, such as deep breathing exercises or brief mindfulness breaks, allow individuals to center themselves and regain focus amid the chaos. These techniques can help ground a person in the present moment, minimizing feelings of anxiety and overwhelm. Additionally, establishing a routine that includes regular breaks can prevent burnout and promote mental clarity, making it easier to tackle tasks without feeling overwhelmed by them.

Nutrition plays an essential role in managing both stress and depression. A balanced diet rich in whole foods, such as fruits, vegetables, whole grains, and lean proteins, can enhance overall well-being. Staying hydrated and avoiding excessive caffeine or sugar can also contribute to mood stability. Preparing healthy meals in advance can reduce the temptation to resort to unhealthy options during busy workdays, thus supporting better mental health. When individuals nourish their bodies adequately, they often find themselves better equipped to handle workplace challenges.

Exercise is another powerful tool for managing workplace stress and alleviating depressive symptoms. Engaging in physical activity releases endorphins, which can improve mood and reduce feelings of stress. Even short bursts of exercise, such as a brisk walk during lunch breaks or stretching exercises at the desk, can make a significant difference in overall mental health. Finding a form of exercise that is enjoyable can encourage consistency, transforming it into a positive outlet rather than another obligation.

Finally, building a robust support system is essential for managing workplace stress while living with depression. Connecting with colleagues or seeking out professional resources, such as counseling or employee assistance programs, can provide valuable emotional support. Open communication about mental health, when appropriate, can foster understanding and empathy among coworkers. By creating an environment where individuals feel safe to discuss their struggles, workplaces can become more compassionate spaces that prioritize mental well-being, ultimately benefiting both employees and the organization as a whole.

Communicating with Employers

Communicating effectively with employers is essential for individuals coping with depression, particularly when the condition impacts daily functioning and performance at work. Transparency can foster understanding and create a supportive environment, but it is important to approach this communication thoughtfully. Begin by assessing your readiness to share your mental health status, as this disclosure can vary in comfort level depending on personal circumstances and the workplace culture. Choose a time when you feel stable and capable of articulating your needs clearly, ensuring that you convey your message without it becoming overwhelming.

When discussing your situation with employers, clarity is key. Be specific about how depression affects your work life, including aspects such as productivity, attendance, and the ability to handle stress. Offer concrete examples to illustrate your experiences, which can help employers understand your perspective. Use language that emphasizes your commitment to your job while expressing the need for accommodations, such as flexible hours or a quieter workspace. Framing your communication in this manner can help employers see that you are striving to balance your mental health with your professional responsibilities.

It is also beneficial to familiarize yourself with your rights regarding mental health in the workplace. Laws such as the Americans with Disabilities Act (ADA) provide certain protections for individuals dealing with mental health issues, allowing for reasonable accommodations. Knowing your rights empowers you to advocate for yourself effectively. Discussing your needs while being aware of these legal frameworks can enhance your confidence and help you navigate conversations with employers more smoothly.

In addition to direct communication, consider utilizing support resources available within your organization. Many workplaces offer Employee Assistance Programs (EAPs) that provide counseling services and mental health resources. Engaging with an EAP can facilitate a dialogue with your employer, as they can help mediate discussions and offer professional insights into your situation. This support can alleviate some pressure by providing expert guidance and reassurance, allowing you to focus on your mental health while maintaining your professional obligations.

Finally, remember that fostering an ongoing dialogue with your employer can create a culture of understanding and support within the workplace. Regular check-ins can help both you and your employer stay aligned on how to manage your needs as they evolve. By maintaining open lines of communication, you contribute to a workplace atmosphere that acknowledges mental health challenges, encouraging others to seek help without fear of stigma. Ultimately, this approach not only benefits you but also paves the way for a more compassionate workplace for everyone.

Finding Support in the Workplace

Finding support in the workplace can be a crucial step for individuals dealing with depression. Many people spend a significant portion of their lives at work, making it an important environment for finding understanding and assistance. Building a support network within your workplace can provide a sense of belonging and security during challenging times. This support can come from colleagues, supervisors, or even human resources departments, who may have resources available for employees facing mental health issues.

Open communication can be a powerful tool in the workplace. Sharing your experiences with trusted coworkers can lead to mutual understanding and support. It's essential to identify individuals who may be empathetic or have had similar experiences. Engaging in conversations about mental health can help reduce stigma and create an atmosphere of acceptance. Additionally, demonstrating vulnerability can encourage others to open up, fostering a community where mental health is prioritized.

Employers also play a key role in creating a supportive environment. Organizations can implement mental health policies, offer employee assistance programs, and provide training for managers on how to recognize and respond to mental health issues. By promoting awareness and education, workplaces can empower employees to seek help and support each other. This proactive approach not only benefits individuals with depression but also enhances overall workplace morale and productivity.

In addition to peer support, utilizing available mental health resources can be beneficial. Many workplaces offer counseling services or access to mental health professionals. Taking advantage of these resources can provide you with coping strategies tailored to your situation. Moreover, participating in workplace wellness programs that focus on stress management, mindfulness, and physical health can further equip you with tools to manage depression and foster resilience.

Lastly, establishing boundaries is essential when navigating work while living with depression. Recognizing your limits and communicating them to supervisors can help create a manageable work environment. It's important to prioritize self-care and seek accommodations when necessary. By taking these steps, you can cultivate a supportive workplace culture that not only acknowledges the challenges of depression but also actively works towards fostering a healthy and productive environment for all employees.

Chapter 9: Understanding the Connection Between Depression and Sleep

The Impact of Sleep on Mental Health

Sleep plays a crucial role in regulating various aspects of mental health, particularly for those grappling with depression. Many individuals suffering from this condition experience disrupted sleep patterns, which can exacerbate their emotional struggles. Research indicates that inadequate sleep can lead to an increase in depressive symptoms, creating a vicious cycle where poor sleep further aggravates mental health issues. Understanding this connection is essential for anyone seeking to manage their depression and improve their overall well-being.

One significant way that sleep affects mental health is through its influence on emotional regulation. During sleep, particularly during the REM stage, the brain processes emotions and memories. For individuals with depression, disrupted sleep can hinder this essential processing, resulting in heightened feelings of sadness, irritability, and anxiety. By prioritizing proper sleep hygiene—such as maintaining a consistent sleep schedule and creating a restful environment—individuals can improve their emotional resilience and better cope with the challenges of depression.

Moreover, sleep deprivation can impact cognitive functions, including concentration, decision-making, and problem-solving abilities. These cognitive impairments can further complicate daily life, making it more challenging to navigate work responsibilities, relationships, and self-care. Consequently, establishing healthy sleep habits can lead to clearer thinking and improved productivity, which may help in managing the daily struggles associated with depression. Simple strategies, like limiting screen time before bed and engaging in relaxing activities, can enhance sleep quality and, in turn, mental clarity.

The relationship between sleep and nutrition is another important aspect to consider. Poor dietary choices can lead to sleep disturbances, while a balanced diet rich in nutrients can promote better sleep quality. Individuals with depression should focus on foods that support brain health, such as omega-3 fatty acids, whole grains, and leafy greens. By aligning their diet with their sleep goals, they can create a more supportive environment for mental health recovery. This holistic approach to managing depression encompasses not only sleep but also nutrition, offering a comprehensive strategy for improvement.

Lastly, mindfulness and meditation techniques can play a significant role in improving sleep quality and, by extension, mental health. Practices such as deep breathing, progressive muscle relaxation, and guided imagery can help individuals calm their minds before bedtime, reducing anxiety that may interfere with sleep. Incorporating these techniques into a daily routine can foster a sense of peace and promote a more restful night's sleep. For those living with depression, recognizing the profound impact of sleep on their mental health can empower them to take proactive steps toward healing and establishing healthier relationships with themselves and others.

Sleep Disorders and Depression

Sleep disorders and depression are intricately linked, with one often exacerbating the other. Many individuals suffering from depression experience sleep disturbances, ranging from insomnia to hypersomnia. Insomnia, characterized by difficulty falling asleep or staying asleep, can lead to increased feelings of anxiety and hopelessness, further aggravating depressive symptoms. Conversely, hypersomnia, or excessive sleeping, can create a cycle of lethargy and disengagement, making it difficult for individuals to participate in daily activities and maintain relationships. Recognizing this connection is vital for managing both sleep and mood effectively.

The impact of sleep disorders on mental health cannot be overstated. Research indicates that poor sleep quality can alter brain function, affecting mood regulation and emotional stability. Furthermore, individuals with depression often have disrupted sleep patterns, including frequent awakenings and non-restorative sleep. This lack of quality rest can lead to a decrease in cognitive functioning, making it harder to cope with daily life challenges. Understanding the mechanisms of sleep can empower individuals to take steps toward improving their rest, which in turn may help alleviate some symptoms of depression.

Coping strategies for addressing sleep disorders involve establishing a consistent sleep routine. Going to bed and waking up at the same time each day can help regulate the body's internal clock. Creating a restful environment is also crucial; minimizing noise, keeping the bedroom dark, and maintaining a comfortable temperature can enhance sleep quality. Additionally, avoiding stimulants such as caffeine and electronic screens before bedtime can prepare the mind and body for rest. Integrating these practices into daily life can significantly improve sleep and provide a foundation for better emotional health.

Nutrition and diet play a critical role in managing both sleep disorders and depression. Certain foods, such as those rich in omega-3 fatty acids, antioxidants, and vitamins, can enhance brain function and promote better sleep. Conversely, heavy or spicy meals close to bedtime may disrupt sleep patterns. Staying hydrated and maintaining balanced blood sugar levels throughout the day can also contribute to improved sleep quality. By being mindful of dietary choices, individuals can create a supportive environment for their mental health.

Lastly, mindfulness and meditation techniques can be powerful tools in addressing both sleep disorders and depression. Practices such as deep breathing, progressive muscle relaxation, and guided imagery can help calm the mind and prepare the body for sleep. Engaging in regular mindfulness exercises can reduce stress and anxiety, making it easier to transition into sleep. Exploring creative outlets, such as journaling or art, can also provide a means of expressing feelings related to depression and serve as a form of emotional release. By integrating these strategies into daily life, individuals can work toward a healthier relationship with sleep and improved overall well-being.

Strategies for Better Sleep Hygiene

Establishing effective sleep hygiene is essential for individuals struggling with depression, as poor sleep can exacerbate depressive symptoms and negatively affect relationships. To improve sleep quality, it is crucial to create a consistent sleep schedule. Going to bed and waking up at the same time each day helps regulate the body's internal clock, making it easier to fall asleep and wake up feeling refreshed. This routine can also enhance mood stability, which is particularly important for those experiencing the emotional turbulence that often accompanies depression.

Creating a restful sleep environment is another vital strategy for better sleep hygiene. The bedroom should be a sanctuary for relaxation, free from distractions such as excessive noise, bright lights, and electronic devices. Consider using blackout curtains to block out light and a white noise machine or earplugs to minimize disturbances. Maintaining a comfortable room temperature can further promote a conducive atmosphere for sleep. This environment fosters a sense of safety and calm, which can be particularly beneficial for individuals dealing with anxiety and restlessness linked to depression.

Incorporating relaxation techniques into the bedtime routine can significantly improve sleep quality. Mindfulness and meditation practices, such as deep breathing exercises or guided imagery, can help quiet the mind and reduce racing thoughts that often accompany depressive episodes. Engaging in calming activities before bed, such as reading a book or taking a warm bath, can signal to the body that it is time to wind down. These practices not only promote better sleep but also provide a constructive outlet for managing stress and emotional pain.

Nutrition plays a crucial role in sleep hygiene and overall mental health. A well-balanced diet, rich in vitamins and minerals, can enhance sleep quality and mood. Certain foods, such as almonds, turkey, and chamomile tea, are known to promote relaxation and improve sleep. Conversely, caffeine and heavy meals close to bedtime can disrupt sleep patterns. Being mindful of dietary choices throughout the day can support better sleep and contribute to overall well-being, helping to mitigate some of the challenges faced by those living with depression.

Lastly, fostering a strong support system is fundamental for individuals navigating depression and its impact on sleep. Connecting with friends, family, or support groups can provide emotional comfort and accountability, encouraging healthier sleep habits. Sharing experiences and coping strategies can lead to valuable insights and motivate individuals to prioritize their sleep hygiene. By building a network of understanding and compassionate individuals, those with depression can feel less isolated, ultimately enhancing their ability to cope with daily challenges and maintain healthier relationships.

Chapter 10: Support Systems and Resources for Individuals with Depression

Building a Support Network

Building a support network is crucial for individuals navigating the complexities of depression. A strong support system can provide emotional comfort, practical assistance, and a sense of belonging, all of which are vital for coping with daily life challenges. Friends, family, and mental health professionals form the backbone of this network. They can offer understanding and encouragement, helping to alleviate feelings of isolation that often accompany depression. Recognizing the importance of these connections is the first step in creating a supportive environment that fosters healing and resilience.

To build an effective support network, it is essential to identify who in your life can provide the understanding and empathy you need. This may include friends who have experience with mental health challenges, family members who are willing to listen, or support groups where individuals share similar experiences. Engaging with these people can help illuminate the path forward and allow you to express your feelings without fear of judgment. Open communication about your struggles is vital, as it helps others to understand your needs and offer the right kind of support.

In addition to personal connections, professional support can play a significant role in managing depression. Therapists, counselors, and support groups can provide strategies tailored to your specific situation, helping you develop coping mechanisms and improve your mental health. Many communities also offer resources such as hotlines or workshops focused on mental health. Seeking out these resources can not only provide immediate relief but also foster long-term strategies for dealing with depression, enhancing your overall quality of life.

Nutrition and physical health also intersect with emotional well-being, making it crucial to incorporate these aspects into your support network. Engaging with dietitians or nutritionists who understand the link between diet and mental health can help you make informed choices that bolster your mood. Similarly, incorporating exercise into your routine can create additional avenues for support, whether through workout buddies or community fitness programs. The combination of emotional support and physical well-being creates a holistic approach to coping with depression.

Lastly, mindfulness and creative outlets can be invaluable components of a support network. Practicing mindfulness techniques can help ground you in the present moment and reduce anxiety, while creative expressions—such as art, writing, or music—offer powerful ways to articulate feelings that may be difficult to verbalize. Engaging in these activities can also connect you with like-minded individuals who share similar struggles, further expanding your support network. By embracing a multifaceted approach to building connections, you can create a robust support system that nurtures your journey through depression.

Professional Help: Therapists and Counselors

Seeking professional help through therapists and counselors can be a vital step in managing depression and its effects on relationships. Mental health professionals are trained to understand the complexities of depression and can provide tailored strategies for coping with daily challenges. They offer a safe space to express feelings and thoughts that may seem overwhelming, helping individuals to process their experiences in a constructive way. By working with a therapist, individuals can develop insight into how depression affects their interactions with loved ones and learn effective communication skills that can enhance their relationships.

Therapists and counselors employ various therapeutic techniques, such as cognitive-behavioral therapy (CBT) and interpersonal therapy (IPT), which are particularly effective for those struggling with depression. CBT focuses on identifying and changing negative thought patterns that contribute to feelings of worthlessness and hopelessness, while IPT emphasizes the importance of improving interpersonal relationships and social functioning. These methods not only help in managing depression but also in fostering healthier connections with partners, family members, and friends.

In addition to traditional talk therapy, many professionals incorporate mindfulness and meditation techniques into their practice. These approaches can empower individuals to develop greater awareness of their thoughts and feelings, enabling them to respond to stressors more effectively. By learning mindfulness strategies, individuals can cultivate a sense of calm and resilience, which is crucial when navigating the emotional turbulence associated with depression. Moreover, counselors can guide clients in finding creative outlets for expressing their feelings, allowing for deeper emotional processing and connection with others.

Nutrition and exercise are other essential components that therapists may address during sessions. Professionals often collaborate with dietitians to help clients understand the link between nutrition and mood. A well-balanced diet can play a significant role in managing depressive symptoms, while exercise has been shown to release endorphins that enhance mood. Counselors can provide practical tips for integrating physical activity into daily routines, helping individuals to find enjoyable forms of exercise that can improve both mental and relational well-being.

Finally, therapists can assist clients in building robust support systems. They can help individuals identify and reach out to friends, family, or support groups that understand the challenges of living with depression. This network can provide emotional support and practical assistance in navigating the complexities of parenting, work, and social interactions while managing depressive symptoms. By fostering connections with others, individuals can create a nurturing environment that encourages healing and strengthens relationships, ultimately leading to a more fulfilling life despite the shadows of depression.

Online Resources and Communities

Online resources and communities have become essential tools for individuals navigating the complexities of depression. These platforms offer a wealth of information and support that can significantly enhance coping strategies in daily life. Websites, forums, and social media groups provide a space for sharing personal experiences, which can help individuals feel less isolated in their struggles. Engaging with these resources can also expose users to new coping techniques, advice on managing symptoms, and insights into how others successfully navigate the challenges of depression.

Nutrition and diet are critical components of managing depression, and various online communities focus specifically on this aspect. Users can find recipes, meal plans, and discussions centered around foods that may help alleviate depressive symptoms. Many platforms also share research and articles that explore the connection between nutrition and mental health, encouraging individuals to adopt healthier eating habits that support their emotional well-being. These resources often emphasize the importance of a balanced diet rich in nutrients, which can contribute to improved mood and energy levels.

Mindfulness and meditation techniques have gained popularity as effective methods for dealing with depression. Online platforms provide guided meditation sessions, instructional videos, and articles that explain the benefits of mindfulness practices. Individuals can join virtual meditation groups or participate in webinars led by mental health professionals. This access to expert guidance can help individuals incorporate mindfulness into their daily routines, providing them with tools to manage stress and anxiety more effectively while fostering a sense of calm and presence.

Creative outlets play a significant role in expressing feelings associated with depression, and numerous online resources encourage artistic expression as a coping strategy. Websites dedicated to art, writing, and music communities allow individuals to showcase their work and connect with others who share similar experiences. These platforms often highlight the therapeutic benefits of creativity, illustrating how engaging in artistic activities can serve as a powerful means of processing emotions and connecting with others. By sharing their creations, individuals may find validation and support from their peers, reinforcing their sense of community.

Support systems are crucial for those living with depression, and the internet has made it easier than ever to find these networks. Online support groups and forums allow individuals to discuss their experiences in a safe environment, offering encouragement and understanding. Many communities also provide resources for parents managing depression while raising children, addressing the unique challenges they face. By connecting with others who understand their struggles, individuals can build a strong support network that fosters resilience, accountability, and hope in their journey toward healing.

Chapter 11: Parenting While Living with Depression

The Challenges of Parenting with Depression

Parenting while dealing with depression presents unique challenges that can impact both the parent and the child. Depression often manifests as persistent sadness, fatigue, and feelings of inadequacy, which can hinder a parent's ability to engage fully with their child. This emotional burden can lead to a cycle of guilt and frustration, as parents may feel they are not meeting their children's needs or living up to their own expectations. Recognizing these feelings is the first step in addressing the challenges that arise from parenting under the shadow of depression.

One significant challenge is the impact of depression on daily routines. Parents may struggle with motivation and energy levels, making it difficult to maintain consistent schedules for activities such as meal times, homework, and bedtime. This inconsistency can create an unstable environment for children, leading to confusion and anxiety. Developing structured routines, even small ones, can provide a sense of normalcy for both the parent and the child. Simple strategies, like preparing meals in advance or setting a regular bedtime, can help mitigate the effects of depression on daily life.

The relationship between a parent and their child can also suffer under the weight of depression. Children are often perceptive to their parents' emotional states, and they may feel the strain of their parent's struggles. This awareness can lead to anxiety, behavioral issues, or even feelings of unworthiness. Open communication is essential in these circumstances. Parents can benefit from discussing their feelings with their children in an age-appropriate way, which can help to foster understanding and reduce stigma surrounding mental health issues.

This dialogue can strengthen the bond between parent and child, creating a supportive atmosphere for both parties.

Nutrition plays a critical role in managing depression and can have a direct impact on parenting. A well-balanced diet not only supports physical health but can also influence mood and energy levels. Parents should aim to incorporate a variety of fruits, vegetables, whole grains, and lean proteins into their meals, as these foods can help stabilize mood and provide sustained energy. Involving children in meal preparation can be a creative outlet and a bonding experience, turning healthy eating into a shared activity that benefits both the parent and the child.

Finally, exercise and mindfulness practices can serve as powerful tools for parents battling depression. Engaging in regular physical activity can boost mood through the release of endorphins, while mindfulness and meditation can help manage stress and improve emotional regulation. Parents might consider incorporating short exercise sessions or mindfulness practices into their daily routines, even if it is just for a few minutes at a time. By prioritizing self-care and finding healthy ways to cope with their own mental health challenges, parents can create a more nurturing environment for their children, ultimately fostering resilience and emotional well-being for the entire family.

Strategies for Maintaining Family Connections

Maintaining family connections can be particularly challenging for those suffering from depression, yet these relationships are vital for emotional support and well-being. One effective strategy is to establish regular communication patterns. This can be as simple as scheduling weekly family check-ins via video calls or phone calls. Consistency in communication helps to reinforce bonds and provides a structured opportunity to share feelings, updates, and experiences. Additionally, setting aside specific times to connect can make it easier to manage the overwhelming feelings that often accompany depression, ensuring that family members remain informed and engaged in each other's lives.

Another crucial strategy involves creating shared activities that cater to the interests and capabilities of all family members. These activities can range from simple board games to collaborative cooking sessions, or even outdoor walks. Engaging in shared interests fosters connection and creates positive experiences that can help lift moods. It is important to choose activities that feel manageable and enjoyable, as forcing oneself into social interaction can sometimes exacerbate feelings of anxiety or isolation. Small, low-pressure gatherings can make a significant difference in maintaining a sense of family unity.

Mindfulness practices can also play a role in strengthening family connections. Encouraging family members to practice mindfulness together can create a supportive environment where everyone learns to express their feelings and cope with stress more effectively. Techniques such as meditation, deep-breathing exercises, or even mindful eating during family meals can enhance awareness and empathy, allowing family members to connect on a deeper emotional level. This shared practice not only boosts individual mental health but also fosters a culture of support and understanding within the family.

Nutrition and shared meal preparation can further enhance family bonds while simultaneously addressing some of the nutritional deficiencies that can accompany depression. Cooking together not only provides an opportunity for family members to work collaboratively but also encourages healthier eating habits, which can positively impact mood and overall mental health. By involving all family members in meal planning and preparation, individuals can express their preferences and engage in meaningful conversations, making mealtime a valued ritual that strengthens familial ties.

Lastly, building a support system that includes family members can be immensely beneficial. Family members can be encouraged to educate themselves about depression, which can help reduce stigma and foster a more supportive atmosphere. Open discussions about mental health can lead to greater understanding and patience among family members. Additionally, establishing family meetings to discuss feelings, challenges, and coping strategies can create an environment where everyone feels heard and valued. This proactive approach not only strengthens connections but also provides a foundation for resilience in the face of depression.

Resources for Parents with Depression

Navigating the challenges of parenting while managing depression can feel overwhelming. It is crucial for parents to access resources that can provide support, education, and practical strategies to cope with the daily demands of parenting. Numerous organizations and online platforms offer invaluable assistance, including mental health hotlines, local support groups, and websites dedicated to mental health awareness. These resources can help parents connect with others who understand their struggles, share coping strategies, and provide a sense of community that can alleviate feelings of isolation.

Incorporating nutrition and diet into daily life is another essential resource for parents dealing with depression. Research indicates that a balanced diet can have a significant impact on mood and overall mental health. Parents can benefit from exploring meal planning resources that focus on nutrient-rich foods that support brain health, such as omega-3 fatty acids, whole grains, and fresh fruits and vegetables. Additionally, workshops and online courses that educate parents on meal preparation and nutritional guidelines can empower them to make healthier choices for themselves and their families.

Mindfulness and meditation techniques serve as powerful tools for managing depression, especially for parents. There are numerous apps and online courses available that guide users through mindfulness practices, breathing exercises, and meditation sessions tailored for those experiencing depressive symptoms. These resources can help parents cultivate a sense of calm, improve emotional regulation, and enhance their ability to connect with their children, ultimately nurturing healthier family dynamics.

Creative outlets can also play a pivotal role in expressing feelings of depression and fostering emotional release. Parents may find relief through various artistic expressions, such as writing, painting, or music. Community art programs, online workshops, and local classes can provide opportunities for parents to explore their creativity while connecting with others who share similar experiences. Engaging in creative activities not only serves as a therapeutic outlet but can also encourage parents to model healthy emotional expression for their children.

Lastly, establishing a robust support system is essential for parents living with depression. This can include reaching out to friends, family members, or professional therapists who understand the complexities of balancing parenting with mental health challenges. Local community centers often host parenting support groups, while online forums and social media platforms can provide a space for parents to share their experiences and gain insights from others. By leveraging these resources, parents can foster resilience, enhance their coping strategies, and ultimately create a nurturing environment for their children, despite the shadows of depression.

www.ingramcontent.com/pod-product-compliance
Lightning Source LLC
Chambersburg PA
CBHW061527250726

48657CB00005B/2113